ICE CREAM COOKBOOK

Easy and Healthy Recipes of Fresh Homemade Ice Creams, Sorbet, Ice Pops and Other Frozen Treats

Kaitlyn Donnelly

COPYRIGHT © 2021 BY KAITLYN DONNELLY

ALL RIGHTS RESERVED.
No part of this book may be reproduced in any form or by any electronic or mechanical means, except in the case of a brief quotation embodied in articles or reviews, without written permission from its publisher.

DISCLAIMER
The recipes and information in this book are provided for educational purposes only. Please always consult a licensed professional before making changes to your lifestyle or diet. The author and publisher shall have neither liability nor responsibility to anyone with respect to any loss or damage caused or alleged to be caused directly or indirectly by the information contained in this book. All trademarks and brands within this book are for clarifying purposes only and are owned by the owners themselves, not affiliated with this document.

Images from shutterstock.com

CONTENTS

INTRODUCTION 5

CHAPTER 1: Ice Cream in a Nutshell 6

CHAPTER 2: Recipes 8

FRUITY ICE CREAM 8

- Blackberry Ice Cream 8
- Blackberry Buttermilk Ice Cream 9
- Blueberry Ice Cream 10
- Creamier Raspberry Ice Cream 11
- Coconut Ice Cream 12
- Creamy Lemon Ice Cream 13
- Peach Ice Cream 14
- Raspberry Ice Cream 15
- Banana Flavored Ice Cream 16
- Strawberry Ice Cream 17
- Strawberry Cheesecake Ice Cream 18
- Strawberry Coconut Ice Cream 19
- Pumpkin Ice Cream 20
- Lime Ice Cream 21

CHOCOLATE ICE CREAM 22

- Simple Chocolate Ice Cream 22
- Chocolate Frosty 23
- Chocolate Avocado Ice Cream 24
- Vegan Chocolate Ice Cream 25
- Cherry Flavored Chocolate Ice Cream 26
- Chunky Nutty Ice Cream 27

OTHER ICE CREAM FLAVORS 28

- Hazelnut Mocha Ice Cream 28
- Peanut Butter Ice Cream 29
- Pecan Ice Cream 30
- Almond Ice Cream 31
- Egg Free Vanilla Ice Cream 32
- Egg Free Green Tea Ice Cream 33
- Creamy Ice Cream 34
- Irish Cream Ice Cream 35
- Mint Chocolate Ice Cream 36
- Coffee Ice Cream 37
- Ziplock Bag Ice Cream 38

FROZEN TREATS 39

- Avocado Sorbet 39
- Fruit Sherbet 40
- Coconut Milk Fudge Pops 41
- Vanilla-Almond Ice Pops 42
- Strawberry Cheesecake Pops 43
- Raspberry Sherbet 44
- Vanilla Bean Semifreddo 45
- Vanilla Sherbet 46
- Apricot Sherbet 47

ICED DRINKS 48

- Iced Tea 48
- Iced Omega Tea 49
- Low-Carb Colada 50
- Fresh Lemonade 51
- Energetic Iced Coffee 52
- Summer Smoothie 53

CONCLUSION 54

RECIPE INDEX 55

CONVERSION TABLES 56

INTRODUCTION

Even the thought of ice cream is enough to conjure dreams of sunny weekend days lounging around in the yard, running through the sprinkler, and taking a break from the heat with a delicious ice-cold treat. While the store-bought stuff is nice, it's not hard to make a batch of really rich, bend-your-spoon thick ice cream without breaking the bank.

Forget what you know about boring and dull desserts. Forget all previous attempts at horribly bad ice cream. In this book you'll find the most delicious recipes for treats on hot summer days. Step-by-step directions and pictures will help you start creating these special desserts in your own kitchen.

CHAPTER 1: ICE CREAM IN A NUTSHELL

To make perfect ice cream, you first need to understand the rules. There are several different basic methods of making ice cream. In this book, nearly all of the recipes are of the French custard style, using egg yolks, sugar and cream. A few of them use gelatine or pectin, instead of eggs, to thicken the mixture; some use both gelatine and egg yolks; one uses a soft cheese. Once you've acquired an understanding of the way levels of fat, solids and liquids can be adjusted to create different tastes and textures, you can create your own flavors.

THE FOUR BASIC STEPS OF MAKING ICE CREAM

The process of making ice cream will vary depending on the ingredients and the style. Here are the basic steps for making a custard-style ice cream; the last three steps are much the same for any kind of ice cream or sorbet.

1. COOKING

This step usually involves cooking milk and cream together in a saucepan, sometimes with the addition of one or more flavorings, such as vanilla. Then, combining egg yolks with sugar to make a thick, glossy paste, incorporating the reheated milk mixture, slowly and carefully, with the egg mixture, and, finally, returning the combined mixture to the pan and cooking it until it reaches a custard-like consistency. To test for this stage, one lifts the mixing spoon out of the mixture and runs a finger over the back of it. If the finger leaves a clear mark, the mixture is ready.

2. COOLING

The cooked mixture needs to be poured into a container of some kind, such as a large jug or bowl, and left to cool to room temperature. Then it is covered and refrigerated for at least an hour to chill. The chilling is an essential step to prepare it for the freezing process.

3. CHURNING

The mixture is transferred to an ice cream maker and left to churn and partially freeze. It is this step, which usually takes 30-40 minutes, that gives the ice cream its smooth, light texture.

4. FREEZING

Transfer the ice cream to a suitable container or an ice cream mold, cover with a lid and place in the freezer to set solid. This will take at least 1 hour. Once removed from the freezer, the ice cream will need to be left for about 15 minutes at room temperature to soften, so that it can be scooped out easily.

MAKING ICE CREAM WITHOUT A MACHINE

Follow steps 1 and 2 above, then place it in a large container, cover it and freeze for 1 hour. Remove the container from the freezer and whisk the mixture vigorously with a fork to aerate it and break up the ice crystals. At this point, add any mix-ins, such as nuts or chocolate chips. Return the ice cream to the freezer for another hour, then remove it and whisk again. Repeat this last step once more, then leave the ice cream in the freezer to set solid. In some cases it may be desirable to whisk it 4 or even 5 times.

CHAPTER 2: RECIPES
FRUITY ICE CREAM
BLACKBERRY ICE CREAM

SERVINGS: 10 | PREP TIME: 30 min. (+ 2 h.) | COOK TIME: 7

CARBS: 4.3 g | FAT: 35 g | PROTEIN: 2 g | CALORIES: 338

INGREDIENTS

- 1 cup blackberries, chopped
- ¾ tsp liquid Splenda
- 1 tsp lemon juice
- 1 tsp vanilla extract
- 4 cups heavy whipping cream

DIRECTIONS

1. Combine the blackberries with lemon juice and Splenda in a large saucepan.
2. Mash the blackberries slightly then bring the mixture to a boil on medium heat, occasionally stirring, about 5 minutes.
3. Transfer to a blender and puree until smooth.
4. Stir in the vanilla and cream, then cover and place in the fridge for 2 hours.
5. Transfer to your ice cream maker. Process according to the manufacturer's directions.

BLACKBERRY BUTTERMILK ICE CREAM

SERVINGS: 10 | PREP TIME: 40 min. | COOK TIME: 35 min.

CARBS: 6 g | FAT: 14 g | PROTEIN: 2 g | CALORIES: 155

INGREDIENTS

- ½ pound blackberries, chopped
- 1 Tbsp water
- 2 Tbsp lemon juice
- ¼ cup erythritol
- 1 pinch ground nutmeg
- ⅛ tsp cinnamon
- ⅛ tsp stevia glycerite
- ¼ tsp vanilla extract
- 1⅛ cups buttermilk
- 1½ cups heavy cream
- ⅓ cup erythritol
- ¼ tsp salt
- 2 Tbsp vodka
- 2 tsp balsamic vinegar
- ½ tsp stevia glycerite

DIRECTIONS

1. In a saucepan, stir together blackberries, water, lemon juice, ¼ cup erythritol, nutmeg and cinnamon.
2. Bring to a simmer on medium heat. Reduce to low heat and simmer for 10 minutes.
3. Transfer to a blender and puree until smooth.
4. Return puree to the saucepan and let simmer uncovered for about 25 minutes, stirring occasionally, until thickened and syrupy.
5. Remove from heat and stir in ⅛ tsp stevia glycerite and vanilla extract. Set aside to cool completely. You can place in the fridge.
6. In a blender, combine blackberry puree, buttermilk, heavy cream, ⅓ cup erythritol, salt, vodka, balsamic vinegar and ½ tsp stevia glycerite. Blend until well mixed.
7. Pour into your ice cream maker. Process according to the manufacturer's directions.

BLUEBERRY ICE CREAM

SERVINGS: 10 | PREP TIME: 30 min. (+ 2 h.) | COOK TIME: 7 min.

CARBS: 4.4 g | FAT: 35 g | PROTEIN: 2 g | CALORIES: 338

INGREDIENTS

- 1 cup blueberries, chopped
- ¾ tsp liquid Splenda
- 1 tsp lemon juice
- 1 tsp vanilla extract
- 4 cups heavy whipping cream

DIRECTIONS

1. Combine the blueberries, lemon juice and Splenda in a large saucepan.
2. Mash the blueberries slightly, then bring the mixture to a boil on medium heat, occasionally stirring, about 5 minutes.
3. Transfer to a blender and puree until smooth.
4. Stir in the vanilla and cream, then cover and place in the fridge for 2 hours.
5. Pour into your ice cream maker. Process according to the manufacturer's directions.

CREAMIER RASPBERRY ICE CREAM

SERVINGS: 8 | PREP TIME: 30 min. (+ 4 h.) | COOK TIME: 20 min.

CARBS: 5 g | FAT: 21 g | PROTEIN: 4 g | CALORIES: 249

INGREDIENTS

- *1 cup unsweetened almond milk*
- *2½ cups heavy cream*
- *½ cup of Swerve sweetener*
- *4 egg yolks*
- *1½ oz of cocoa butter, chopped*
- *1 tsp vanilla extract*
- *2 Tbsp vodka*
- *½ tsp xanthan gum*
- *¼ tsp of liquid stevia extract*
- *1½ cups of frozen raspberries*

DIRECTIONS

1. Add some water to a large bowl then fill with ice cubes. Place a medium bowl inside large bowl.
2. In a saucepan, mix almond milk and cream. Place on medium-low heat then stir in Swerve until it dissolves and the mixture becomes hot.
3. Whisk the egg yolks in a bowl.
4. Whisk ½ cup of the hot cream into the egg mixture, then whisk the egg mixture into the hot cream on the stove. Whisk continuously until the mixture is hot.
5. After removing, stir in the cocoa butter.
6. Pour into the bowl set in ice, then let cool for about 10 minutes.
7. Wrap the bowl with plastic wrap and place in the fridge for at least 4 hours.
8. Stir in vanilla extract, vodka, xanthan gum and stevia extract.
9. Transfer to an ice cream maker and process according to the machine instructions.
10. Serve with the frozen raspberries.

COCONUT ICE CREAM

SERVINGS: 8 | PREP TIME: 30 min. (+ 2 h.) | COOK TIME: 20 min.

CARBS: 4.5 g | FAT: 26 g | PROTEIN: 3 g | CALORIES: 258

INGREDIENTS

- ½ cup unsweetened coconut flakes, toasted
- 1 cup coconut cream
- 1 cup heavy cream
- 4 egg yolks
- 6 drops liquid Splenda
- 2 Tbsp xylitol
- 1 Tbsp vanilla extract

DIRECTIONS

1. In a saucepan, combine coconut cream, heavy cream and coconut flakes. Bring to a simmer over low heat and set aside to steep for about 10 minutes.
2. Combine egg yolks, Splenda and xylitol in a bowl. Beat for a few seconds.
3. Add the hot cream mixture to the egg mixture and return all to the saucepan on low heat. Beat until thick.
4. Remove from heat and add vanilla extract. Beat for a few seconds more.
5. Cover and chill immediately over an ice bath. Chill in the fridge for 2 hours.
6. Churn in your ice cream machine according to manufacturer's instructions.

CREAMY LEMON ICE CREAM

SERVINGS: 2 | PREP TIME: 5 min. (+ 2 h.) | COOK TIME: none

CARBS: 2.7 g | FAT: 34 g | PROTEIN: 4.3 g | CALORIES: 344

INGREDIENTS

- 3 oz cream cheese, softened
- 2 Tbsp lemon juice
- 2 tsp Erythritol
- 1 cup whipped cream

DIRECTIONS

1. Combine cream cheese, lemon juice and Erythritol in a blender. Blend for 5 seconds.
2. Gently stir in the whipped cream, then transfer to a dish.
3. Place in refrigerator until firm, at least 2 hours. Serve.

PEACH ICE CREAM

SERVINGS: 8 | PREP TIME: 30 min. (+ 2 h.) | COOK TIME: 20 min.

CARBS: 4.2 g | FAT: 16.5 g | PROTEIN: 2.9 g | CALORIES: 171

INGREDIENTS

- ¾ cup half and half
- 4 egg yolks
- 8 drops liquid Splenda
- 3 Tbsp xylitol
- 1 cup heavy whipping cream
- 1 cup peaches, peeled, chopped

DIRECTIONS

1. Bring half and half to a simmer in the top of a double boiler over medium heat.
2. Meanwhile, in a mixing bowl, beat together egg yolks and sweeteners.
3. Whisk a little amount of the hot half and half into egg mixture.
4. Return all to the top of a double boiler and whisk into the remaining half and half. Cook, constantly stirring, until thick, about 12-15 minutes.
5. Remove from heat and stir in the heavy cream.
6. Place in freezer for at least 2 hours.
7. Puree peaches in a blender and stir into the cream base.
8. Transfer to your ice cream maker and process, following directions from the manufacturer.

RASPBERRY ICE CREAM

SERVINGS: 8 | PREP TIME: 30 min. (+ 1 h.) | COOK TIME: 20 min.

CARBS: 5.1 g | FAT: 27.4 g | PROTEIN: 2.7 g | CALORIES: 420

INGREDIENTS

- 1 cup raspberries (fresh or frozen, thawed)
- ¾ tsp liquid Splenda
- 2 Tbsp lemon juice
- 1 tsp vanilla extract
- 4 cups heavy whipping cream

DIRECTIONS

1. Combine raspberries, Splenda and lemon juice in a medium saucepan.
2. Bring to a boil on medium heat, occasionally stirring and slightly mashing the berries, about 5 minutes.
3. Transfer to a blender, blend, then set aside to cool for about 1 hour.
4. Stir in the vanilla and heavy cream.
5. Process in your ice cream maker, following machine directions.

BANANA FLAVORED ICE CREAM

SERVINGS: 8 | PREP TIME: 25 min. (+ 2 h.) | COOK TIME: none

CARBS: 1.7 g | FAT: 23 g | PROTEIN: 1.2 g | CALORIES: 213

INGREDIENTS

- *2 Tbsp banana extract*
- *1 cup unsweetened coconut milk*
- *2 cups heavy whipping cream*
- *1 tsp Vanilla extract*
- *3 squeezes sucralose sweetener*

DIRECTIONS

1. In a bowl, combine all ingredients and stir well.
2. Transfer to the ice cream machine and churn for 25 minutes.
3. Place in your freezer to chill for at least 2 hours.

STRAWBERRY ICE CREAM

SERVINGS: 8 | PREP TIME: 25 min. | COOK TIME: none

CARBS: 6 g | FAT: 20 g | PROTEIN: 1.4 g | CALORIES: 202

INGREDIENTS

- *2 cups heavy cream*
- *1 cup almond milk*
- *2 cups frozen strawberries*
- *¼ cup Splenda*
- *1 tsp vanilla extract*

DIRECTIONS

1. Combine the ingredients in a blender and blend until smooth.
2. Transfer to ice cream maker and process, following the instructions of the manufacturer.

STRAWBERRY CHEESECAKE ICE CREAM

SERVINGS: 8 | PREP TIME: 30 min. (+ 2 h.) | COOK TIME: 10 min.

CARBS: 4 g | FAT: 35 g | PROTEIN: 3.5 g | CALORIES: 347

INGREDIENTS

- *5 oz strawberries, sliced*
- *2 Tbsp butter*
- *3 Tbsp Swerve*
- *8 oz cream cheese*
- *2 cups heavy cream*
- *¾ cup Swerve*
- *½ tsp vanilla*
- *Juice from 1 lemon*

DIRECTIONS

1. Mix together strawberries, butter and 3 Tbsp Swerve in a small saucepan on medium heat.
2. Bring to a simmer and cook for 5-6 minutes.
3. Set aside until completely cool, about 2 hours.
4. In a mixing bowl, beat the cream cheese until smooth.
5. Add the heavy cream, ¾ cup Swerve, vanilla and lemon juice. Mix until the mixture thickens and cream cheese is incorporated thoroughly into the cream, about 2-3 minutes.
6. Transfer to an ice cream maker and process according to the instructions.
7. Serve with the strawberries mixture.

STRAWBERRY COCONUT ICE CREAM

SERVINGS: 8 | PREP TIME: 20 min. (+ 1 h.) | COOK TIME: none

CARBS: 4.3 g | FAT: 20.4 g | PROTEIN: 2 g | CALORIES: 194

INGREDIENTS

- 1 cup strawberries, sliced
- 2 (13.5-ounce) cans coconut milk
- ½ tsp coconut flavored liquid stevia
- ½ cup Swerve

DIRECTIONS

1. Combine all ingredients in your blender and puree until smooth.
2. Pour into your ice cream maker. Process according to the manufacturer's directions.
3. Freeze for about 1 hour before you serve.

PUMPKIN ICE CREAM

SERVINGS: 12 | PREP TIME: 40 min. (+ 2 h.) | COOK TIME: 20 min.

CARBS: 2.6 g | FAT: 17 g | PROTEIN: 2.3 g | CALORIES: 185

INGREDIENTS

- 1 cup canned salt-free pumpkin
- 1 tsp vanilla extract
- 2 cups heavy cream
- 5 large egg yolks
- 1 pinch stevia
- ⅓ cup xylitol
- ⅛ tsp ground nutmeg
- ¾ tsp ground ginger
- ¾ tsp ground cinnamon
- ¼ tsp salt

DIRECTIONS

1. Add pumpkin and vanilla to a small bowl, then place in the fridge for 2 hours.
2. Whisk egg yolks with ½ cup of heavy cream in a small bowl and set aside.
3. In a saucepan, combine the remaining heavy cream, stevia, xylitol, nutmeg, ginger, cinnamon and salt. Heat on medium until it just starts to simmer, then remove from heat.
4. Whisk the hot mixture slowly into the egg yolk mixture until incorporated.
5. Return everything to the saucepan and cook on medium heat, constantly stirring, until the mixture slightly thickens. Do not let boil.
6. Remove from heat and stir the pumpkin and vanilla.
7. Cool in an ice bath, then place in fridge to chill for at least 4 hours.
8. Transfer to the ice cream maker and process according to the directions of the machine.

LIME ICE CREAM

SERVINGS: 3 | PREP TIME: 15 min. (+ 10 h.) | COOK TIME: none

CARBS: 5 g | FAT: 17.7 g | PROTEIN: 2.4 g | CALORIES: 179

INGREDIENTS

- *1 cup whipped cream*
- *½ cup almond milk*
- *2 Tbsp lime zest*
- *1 tsp lime juice*
- *2 Tbsp almonds, chopped*

DIRECTIONS

1. Combine whipped cream with milk and stir carefully.
2. Add lime zest and lime juice and stir it again.
3. Add the mixture to a container and freeze for 10 hours.
4. Sprinkle with the chopped almonds.

CHOCOLATE ICE CREAM
SIMPLE CHOCOLATE ICE CREAM

SERVINGS: 3 | PREP TIME: 30 min. (+ 1 h.) | COOK TIME: none

CARBS: 3.4 g | FAT: 35 g | PROTEIN: 8.7 g | CALORIES: 355

INGREDIENTS

- 2 eggs
- 1 cup heavy cream
- ⅓ cup Swerve
- 1 tsp vanilla extract
- ¼ cup dark cocoa powder

DIRECTIONS

1. Combine everything in your blender then puree until smooth.
2. Pour into your ice cream maker. Process according to the manufacturer's directions.
3. Freeze for about 1 hour before you serve.

CHOCOLATE FROSTY

SERVINGS: 3 | PREP TIME: 10 min. (+ 30 min.) | COOK TIME: none

CARBS: 2.2 g | FAT: 22.5 g | PROTEIN: 1.3 g | CALORIES: 238

INGREDIENTS

- *1 cup heavy cream*
- *1 tsp vanilla extract*
- *⅓ cup sugar-free cocoa mix*

DIRECTIONS

1. In a mixing bowl, beat together heavy cream and vanilla until soft peaks just start to form.
2. Add the cocoa gradually until fully combined. Beat for about 30 seconds more, or until stiff peaks form.
3. Place in the freezer for 30 minutes.

CHOCOLATE AVOCADO ICE CREAM

SERVINGS: 6 | PREP TIME: 25 min. (+ 6 h. 30 min.) | COOK TIME: none

CARBS: 3.7 g | FAT: 22.8 g | PROTEIN: 3 g | CALORIES: 241

INGREDIENTS

- *2 ripe avocados*
- *⅙ cup heavy cream*
- *1 cup coconut milk*
- *2 tsp vanilla extract*
- *½ cup cocoa powder*
- *25 drops of liquid stevia*
- *½ cup powdered erythritol*
- *6 squares of unsweetened baker's chocolate, chopped*

DIRECTIONS

1. In a deep bowl, combine avocado, heavy cream, coconut milk and vanilla extract.
2. Blend until smooth, using an immersion blender.
3. Add cocoa powder, stevia and erythritol, then blend again.
4. Fold in the chopped squares of chocolate.
5. Place the bowl in the refrigerator for at least 6 hours, or overnight.
6. Process in your ice cream machine according to the manufacturer's instructions.
7. Place in freezer for at least 30 minutes before serving.

VEGAN CHOCOLATE ICE CREAM

SERVINGS: 6 | PREP TIME: 25 min. | COOK TIME: none

CARBS: 3.4 g | FAT: 16 g | PROTEIN: 2 g | CALORIES: 160

INGREDIENTS

- ½ cup unsweetened almond milk
- 1 (15-ounce) can coconut milk
- 2 Tbsp unsweetened cocoa powder
- 2 Tbsp xylitol

DIRECTIONS

1. Combine all ingredients in a bowl and whisk together thoroughly.
2. Transfer to your ice cream maker and process according to the instructions of the manufacturer.

CHERRY FLAVORED CHOCOLATE ICE CREAM

SERVINGS: 6 | PREP TIME: 30 min. | COOK TIME: none

CARBS: 3.9 g | FAT: 13.8 g | PROTEIN: 2 g | CALORIES: 150

INGREDIENTS

- 1¾ cup coconut milk
- 1 Tbsp cherry flavoring
- ½ cup powdered erythritol
- ⅓ cup dark chocolate, grated
- ¼ cup unsweetened cocoa powder

DIRECTIONS

1. In a bowl, mix together the coconut milk, erythritol and cherry flavoring.
2. Stir in the grated chocolate and cocoa powder.
3. Transfer to an ice cream maker and process according to machine instructions.

CHUNKY NUTTY ICE CREAM

SERVINGS: 6 | PREP TIME: 30 min. (+ 5-6 h.) | COOK TIME: none

CARBS: 7.6 g | FAT: 29 g | PROTEIN: 5.5 g | CALORIES: 285

INGREDIENTS

- ¼ cup 85% Dark chocolate, chopped coarsely
- ¼ cup unsalted macadamia nuts, chopped coarsely
- ¼ cup walnuts, chopped coarsely
- ¼ cup chopped pecan halves
- 1 cup unsweetened Vanilla almond milk
- 4 oz unsweetened chocolate, chopped
- 2 large eggs
- 1 cup Swerve
- 1 cup heavy cream
- 2 Tbsp vodka
- ½ tsp xanthan gum
- 1 tsp vanilla extract
- 1 pinch salt

DIRECTIONS

1. In a bowl, combine dark chocolate, macadamia nuts, walnuts and pecans. Cover and place in the fridge for 1 hour.
2. Add unsweetened chocolate to a microwave safe bowl. Microwave until melted, bringing it out every 30 seconds to stir.
3. Add the almond milk to the chocolate. Microwave and stir in 30 seconds intervals until smooth. Place in the refrigerator to cool for 2 hours.
4. In a separate bowl, whisk the eggs until light and fluffy.
5. Gradually whisk in the Swerve until blended.
6. Add the heavy cream, vodka, xanthan gum, vanilla and salt. Whisk until blended.
7. Stir in the chocolate and almond milk mixture.
8. Cover and place in the fridge for 2-3 hours.
9. Transfer to an ice cream maker and process according to the machine instructions.
10. Add the dark chocolate and nut mixture in the last few minutes of churning.

OTHER ICE CREAM FLAVORS
HAZELNUT MOCHA ICE CREAM

SERVINGS: 6 | PREP TIME: 30 min. (+ 4 h.) | COOK TIME: none

CARBS: 6.3 g | FAT: 34 g | PROTEIN: 4.7 g | CALORIES: 341

INGREDIENTS

- 3½ cups heavy cream
- 3 tsp instant decaffeinated coffee granules
- ⅓ cup unsweetened cocoa powder
- 3 oz unsweetened baking chocolate squares
- 6 large egg yolks
- 1 cup Splenda
- 1 Tbsp vanilla extract
- ⅓ cup chopped hazelnuts

DIRECTIONS

1. Add heavy cream, coffee granules, cocoa powder and chocolate squares to a medium saucepan. Cook on medium-low heat, occasionally stirring, until the mixture starts to simmer and the chocolate has melted.
2. Remove from heat and let cool then whisk until smooth.
3. Combine egg yolks and Splenda in a medium bowl and whisk together.
4. Whisk 1 cup of the chocolate mixture into the egg yolks mixture, then pour all back into the saucepan.
5. Cook on medium-low heat, constantly stirring, until the mixture slightly thickens. Do not let boil.
6. Remove from heat and stir in vanilla.
7. Cover then place in fridge to chill for at least 4 hours.
8. Transfer to the ice cream maker and process according to the directions of the machine.
9. Add the chopped hazelnuts in the last few minutes of churning.

PEANUT BUTTER ICE CREAM

SERVINGS: 8 | PREP TIME: 20 min. (+ 4 h.) | COOK TIME: 15 min.

CARBS: 4.5 g | FAT: 22.7 g | PROTEIN: 7.5 g | CALORIES: 422

INGREDIENTS

- 3 cups heavy whipping cream
- 2 eggs
- ¼ tsp liquid Splenda
- ½ cup peanut butter
- ½ tsp vanilla extract

DIRECTIONS

1. In a medium pot, simmer heavy cream until hot, about 3-4 minutes. Remove from heat.
2. In a bowl, whisk eggs and Splenda until fluffy.
3. Whisk a little heavy cream slowly into the egg, then whisk the egg into the heavy cream in the pot.
4. Cook gently on medium-low heat, constantly stirring, until thick.
5. Strain into a bowl through a fine-mesh sieve.
6. Whisk in the vanilla and peanut butter.
7. Let the mixture cool to room temperature, then transfer to refrigerator to chill for at least 4 hours.
8. Transfer to your ice cream maker and process according to the instructions.

PECAN ICE CREAM

SERVINGS: 8 | PREP TIME: 20 min. (+ 1 h.) | COOK TIME: 15 min.

CARBS: 4.4 g | FAT: 51 g | PROTEIN: 3 g | CALORIES: 482

INGREDIENTS

- *4 cups heavy whipping cream*
- *2 Tbsp butter*
- *½ tsp liquid Splenda*
- *1 tsp vanilla extract*
- *½ cup chopped pecans, toasted*

DIRECTIONS

1. In a saucepan, combine 2 cups heavy cream, butter and Splenda.
2. Cook on low, stirring until bubbly.
3. Remove from heat, let cool for 1 hour, then transfer to the ice cream maker.
4. Stir in the vanilla and remaining 2 cups heavy cream.
5. Process according to the instructions of the ice cream machine.
6. Add pecans when the ice cream starts to harden.

ALMOND ICE CREAM

SERVINGS: 2 | PREP TIME: 20 min. (+ 7 h.) | COOK TIME: none

CARBS: 12 g | FAT: 11.4 g | PROTEIN: 2.2 g | CALORIES: 158

INGREDIENTS

- 1½ cup almond milk
- 3½ oz Swerve sweetener
- 3½ oz double cream
- 3 Tbsp liquid stevia
- 3 Tbsp almonds, chopper
- 1 tsp vanilla extract
- 1 Tbsp almonds flakes

DIRECTIONS

1. Whisk double cream to form strong peaks.
2. Add almond milk.
3. Add vanilla extract and stevia. Stir carefully.
4. Add sweetener.
5. Transfer the mixture to a container and freeze for 7 hours.
6. Serve with almonds flakes.

EGG FREE VANILLA ICE CREAM

SERVINGS: 10 | PREP TIME: 45 min. (+ 2 h.) | COOK TIME: 7 min.

CARBS: 1.9 g | FAT: 11.5 g | PROTEIN: 1.1 g | CALORIES: 127

INGREDIENTS

- 1 cups heavy cream
- 1 cup half and half
- 1 tsp granulated sucralose
- ½ cup granulated erythritol
- ½ tsp xanthan gum
- 1½ Tbsp glycerin
- 2 tsp vodka
- 1 tsp vanilla extract

DIRECTIONS

1. In a saucepan, combine heavy cream, half and half, erythritol, sucralose and xanthan gum.
2. Bring to a boil over medium heat, then blend with a hand-held mixer.
3. Set aside to cool to room temperature.
4. Stir in glycerin, vodka and vanilla.
5. Transfer to refrigerator to cool for 2 hours.
6. Churn for about 40 to 45 minutes in the ice cream mixer.
7. Freeze according to instructions.

EGG FREE GREEN TEA ICE CREAM

SERVINGS: 5 | PREP TIME: 10 min. (+ 7 h.) | COOK TIME: 30 min.

CARBS: 2.2 g | FAT: 26 g | PROTEIN: 1.5 g | CALORIES: 249

INGREDIENTS

- ⅓ cup boiling water
- 4 green tea bags
- ½ cup sweetener
- 1½ cup heavy cream
- ½ cup almond milk

DIRECTIONS

1. Place tea bags in a cup, then pour boiling water over them.
2. Let steep for about 5 minutes. Squeeze the tea bags and discard.
3. Stir sweetener into the hot tea, then set aside to cool for 1-2 hours.
4. Stir in the heavy cream and almond milk.
5. Transfer to your ice cream maker and process, following directions from the manufacturer.

CREAMY ICE CREAM

SERVINGS: 3 | PREP TIME: 10 min. (+ 10 h. 30 min.) | COOK TIME: 5 min.

CARBS: 1.7 g | FAT: 16.8 g | PROTEIN: 3.4 g | CALORIES: 173

INGREDIENTS

- ½ cup double cream
- 1 tsp vanilla extract
- 3 tsp liquid stevia
- 3 egg yolks

DIRECTIONS

1. Whisk the egg yolks until they are the color of a lemon.
2. Combine double cream, vanilla extract and liquid stevia in a pot and bring to a boil, stirring constantly. It will thicken in 6 minutes.
3. Add whipped egg yolks to the warm cream mixture slowly. Stir very carefully.
4. Chill the mixture for 30 minutes. Then mix with the help of hand mixer.
5. Transfer to a container and freeze for 10 hours.

IRISH CREAM ICE CREAM

SERVINGS: 6 | PREP TIME: 10 min. (+ 10 h. 30 min.) | COOK TIME: 5 min.

CARBS: 4.3 g | FAT: 21.5 g | PROTEIN: 4.8 g | CALORIES: 226

INGREDIENTS

- *4 eggs, beaten*
- *4 tsp sugar-free chocolate syrup*
- *3 tsp stevia*
- *½ cup low-curb Irish cream syrup*
- *1½ cup double cream*
- *1 tsp glucomannan powder*

DIRECTIONS

1. In a pot, whisk together the stevia and double cream.
2. Add Irish cream syrup and chocolate syrup.
3. Bring to a boil, stirring constantly.
4. Add egg slowly.
5. Stir in glucomannan powder and cook 3 minutes more.
6. Chill the mixture for 30 minutes and transfer to a plastic container.
7. Freeze for 10 hours.

MINT CHOCOLATE ICE CREAM

SERVINGS: 8 | PREP TIME: 40 min. (+ 1 h.) | COOK TIME: none

CARBS: 5.7 g | FAT: 25.4 g | PROTEIN: 3.6 g | CALORIES: 268

INGREDIENTS

- 2 ripe avocados
- 2 cups of coconut milk
- 15 drops of Stevia extract
- ½ cup powdered Erythritol
- ½ Tbsp mint extract
- 1 Tbsp vanilla extract
- 1 (3.5-ounce) bar dark 85% chocolate, chopped

DIRECTIONS

1. Add avocado, coconut milk, Stevia, Erythritol, mint extract and vanilla extract to a blender and blend until smooth.
2. Transfer to your ice cream maker and process according to directions from the manufacturer.
3. Serve with the chopped chocolate.
4. Scoop into serving containers and place in the freezer for 45-60 minutes before serving.

COFFEE ICE CREAM

SERVINGS: 4 | PREP TIME: 20 min. | COOK TIME: none

CARBS: 3 g | FAT: 18 g | PROTEIN: 2 g | CALORIES: 181

INGREDIENTS

- ½ cup strong brewed coffee, chilled
- 2 cups heavy whipping cream
- 2 tsp arrowroot powder
- 1 tsp liquid stevia
- 1 tsp vanilla extract

DIRECTIONS

1. Combine all ingredients in a bowl and whisk together.
2. Pour into the ice cream maker. Process according to the instructions of the manufacturer.

ZIPLOCK BAG ICE CREAM

SERVINGS: 2 | PREP TIME: 15 min. | COOK TIME: none

CARBS: 4.2 g | FAT: 22.3 g | PROTEIN: 1.8 g | CALORIES: 218

INGREDIENTS

- *1 cup heavy cream*
- *2 Tbsp milk*
- *1 dash of salt*
- *1 tsp Truvia*
- *1 tsp vanilla extract*

DIRECTIONS

1. Add all ingredients together to a ziplock bag (9"×12").
2. Close the bag securely, forcing out as much air as possible. Shake to mix the contents.
3. Add 3 cups of ice and 2 Tbsp of salt to a larger ziplock.
4. Place the smaller ziplock (6"×9").inside the larger bag and close securely, forcing out as much air as possible.
5. Shake for 4-5 minutes, or until you get desired consistency.

FROZEN TREATS
AVOCADO SORBET

SERVINGS: 4 | PREP TIME: 30 min. (+ 9 h. 25 min.) | COOK TIME: none

CARBS: 11.8 g | FAT: 31.5 g | PROTEIN: 3.1 g | CALORIES: 322

INGREDIENTS

- *2 avocado*
- *1 cup almond milk*
- *1 tsp mango extract*
- *1 tsp Swerve sweetener*

DIRECTIONS

1. Stir to combine all ingredients . If you want to a softer consistency, use hand mixer. It will make your ice cream fluffy as a cloud.
2. Put the ice cream in the ice cream maker and freeze for 25 minutes.
3. Remove the mixture and mix it with hand mixer.
4. Transfer the mixture to a container and freeze for 9 hours, or until firm.

You can also make this dessert without the ice cream maker. For this you need take a bowl with cold water and ice cubes. Put the ice cream in a separate bowl and sest in the ice water bowl. Mix for 20 minutes.

FRUIT SHERBET

SERVINGS: 2 | PREP TIME: 10 min. (+ 9 h.) | COOK TIME: none

CARBS: 3.7 g | FAT: 15.6 g | PROTEIN: 1.3 g | CALORIES: 155

INGREDIENTS

- ½ cup low fat whipped cream
- ¼ cup mashed fruits of your choice
- 3 tsp stevia
- 1 tsp orange juice

DIRECTIONS

1. Combine whipped cream with mashed fruits.
2. Mix 1 tsp of stevia with orange juice.
3. Combine orange juice and cream mixture.
4. Transfer the mixture to a container and freeze for 9 hours or until firm.

COCONUT MILK FUDGE POPS

SERVINGS: 6 | PREP TIME: 10 min. (+ 5 h.) | COOK TIME: 5 min.

CARBS: 4.6 g | FAT: 12.9 g | PROTEIN: 2.2 g | CALORIES: 137

INGREDIENTS

- 1 (13.5-ounce) can full-fat coconut milk
- ⅓ cup cocoa powder
- ⅓ cup powdered erythritol-based sweetener
- Pinch of salt
- 1½ tsp vanilla extract

DIRECTIONS

1. In a saucepan over medium heat, whisk the coconut milk, cocoa powder, sweetener, and salt.
2. Bring to a simmer, whisking constantly.
3. Simmer for 4 to 5 minutes.
4. Whisk in the vanilla extract and remove from heat. Let cool for 10 minutes.
5. Pour into the ice pop molds.
6. Freeze for 1 hour, then push a stick about two-thirds of the way into each mold.
7. Freeze for at least 5 more hours.
8. To unmold, run under hot water for 20 to 30 seconds, then twist the stick gently to release.

VANILLA-ALMOND ICE POPS

SERVINGS: 6 | PREP TIME: 10 min. (+ 6 h.) | COOK TIME: 5 min.

CARBS: 4.2 g | FAT: 14 g | PROTEIN: 3.1 g | CALORIES: 163

INGREDIENTS

- *2 cups almond milk*
- *1 cup heavy whipping cream*
- *1 vanilla bean, halved lengthwise*
- *1 cup shredded unsweetened coconut*

DIRECTIONS

1. Place a saucepan over medium heat and add the almond milk, heavy cream and vanilla bean.
2. Bring the liquid to a simmer. Continue to simmer on low for 5 minutes.
3. Let the liquid cool for 2 hours.
4. Take the vanilla bean out of the liquid and use a knife to scrape the seeds out of the bean into the liquid.
5. Stir in the coconut and divide the liquid between the ice pop molds.
6. Freeze until solid, about 4 hours, and enjoy.

STRAWBERRY CHEESECAKE POPS

SERVINGS: 6 | PREP TIME: 10 min. (+ 4 h.) | COOK TIME: none

CARBS: 3.7 g | FAT: 20.5 g | PROTEIN: 2.4 g | CALORIES: 219

INGREDIENTS

- 4 oz cream cheese, softened
- ½ cup heavy whipping cream
- ¼ cup plus 2 Tbsp powdered erythritol-based sweetener
- 1 tsp grated lemon zest
- 2 tsp fresh lemon juice
- 1 cup chopped strawberries, divided

DIRECTIONS

1. Place the cream cheese in a food processor or high-powered blender and process until smooth.
2. Add the cream, sweetener, lemon zest, and lemon juice. Process until well combined.
3. Add ¾ cup of the strawberries and process until almost fully smooth.
4. Stir in the remaining chopped strawberries.
5. Pour the mixture into the ice pop molds and push a stick about two-thirds of the way into each mold.
6. Freeze for at least 4 hours.
7. To unmold, run under hot water for 20 to 30 seconds, then twist the stick gently to release.

RASPBERRY SHERBET

SERVINGS: 1 | PREP TIME: 20 min. (+ 2 h. 35 min.) | COOK TIME: none

CARBS: 11.8 g | FAT: 17.3 g | PROTEIN: 2.6 g | CALORIES: 204

INGREDIENTS

- ½ cup low-fat whipped cream
- ¼ cup coconut milk
- ¼ cup raspberries
- 3 tsp stevia

DIRECTIONS

1. Puree from raspberries.
2. Stir to combine whipped cream and coconut milk. If you use a whisk, it will cream the mixture without strong peaks.
3. Add teaspoon of stevia.
4. Combine raspberry puree and cream mixture together.
5. Put the sherbet in a container and freeze for 35 minutes.
6. Blend sherbet until it resembles ice chunks.
7. Place sherbet back in the freezer for 2 hours.

VANILLA BEAN SEMIFREDDO

SERVINGS: 3 | PREP TIME: 20 min. (+ 6-8 h.) | COOK TIME: none

CARBS: 2 g | FAT: 22.2 g | PROTEIN: 4.5 g | CALORIES: 245

INGREDIENTS

- 2 large eggs
- 3 large egg yolks
- ⅔ cup powdered erythritol-based sweetener, divided
- 1 Tbsp vodka
- ½ vanilla bean
- 1⅓ cups heavy whipping cream
- ½ tsp vanilla extract

DIRECTIONS

1. Place the eggs, egg yolks, and ⅓ cup of the sweetener in a heatproof bowl set over a pan of barely simmering water.
2. Whisk continuously until the mixture thickens, 5 to 7 minutes.
3. Remove the bowl from the pan and let the mixture cool to lukewarm, whisking frequently.
4. Whisk in the vodka.
5. Slice the vanilla bean open lengthwise and scrape out the seeds using a sharp knife. Stir the vanilla seeds into the egg mixture.
6. In a separate bowl, use an electric mixer to whip the cream with the remaining ⅓ cup of sweetener and the vanilla extract until it holds stiff peaks.
7. Add the egg mixture to the whipped cream and gently fold in until no streaks remain.
8. Transfer the mixture to an airtight container and freeze until firm, 6 to 8 hours.

VANILLA SHERBET

SERVINGS: 3 | PREP TIME: 30 min. (+ 5 h.) | COOK TIME: none

CARBS: 20 g | FAT: 7.7 g | PROTEIN: 2 g | CALORIES: 157

INGREDIENTS

- *1 cup half and half*
- *2 tsp vanilla extract*
- *2 Tbsp sugar*

DIRECTIONS

1. Whisk half and half with sugar.
2. Add vanilla extract and stir carefully.
3. Put the mixture in a container and freeze for 1 hour.
4. Remove from freezer and blend until thick.
5. Place sherbet back in the freezer.
6. Repeat this process every hour for 4 hours.

APRICOT SHERBET

SERVINGS: 2 | PREP TIME: 30 min. (+ 5 h. 30 min.) | COOK TIME: none

CARBS: 8.2 g | FAT: 11.4 g | PROTEIN: 2.2 g | CALORIES: 158

INGREDIENTS

- ½ cup apricot puree
- 3½ oz low-fat cream
- 2 tsp stevia
- 1 tsp vanilla extract

DIRECTIONS

1. Whisk low-fat cream until it looks like liquid sour cream.
2. Add the apricot puree and stir carefully.
3. Add the stevia and vanilla extract.
4. Put the mixture in the ice cream maker and freeze it for 30 minutes.
5. If you want it thicker, you can put to the freezer for 5 more hours.

ICED DRINKS
ICED TEA

SERVINGS: 2 | PREP TIME: 5 min | COOK TIME: none

CARBS: 0.8 g | FAT: 0 g | PROTEIN: 0 g | CALORIES: 3

INGREDIENTS

- 2 cups chilled brewed tea
- 1 Tbsp apple cider vinegar
- 8 drops liquid stevia
- 2 to 4 ice cubes, for serving

DIRECTIONS

1. Place all the ingredients except the ice in a 16-ounce or larger glass jar, such as a mason jar. Cover and give it a little shake.
2. When ready to consume, transfer to a large drinking glass and add the ice.

ICED OMEGA TEA

SERVINGS: 2 | PREP TIME: 5 min. | COOK TIME: none

CARBS: 5 g | FAT: 19 g | PROTEIN: 4.8 g | CALORIES: 212

INGREDIENTS

- 5 cups chilled brewed green tea
- ¼ cup flavored flax oil or fish oil blend
- ¼ cup collagen peptides or protein powder
- ¼ cup MCT oil
- 8 to 10 drops liquid stevia (optional)
- 8 ice cubes, for serving

DIRECTIONS

1. Place the green tea, fish oil, collagen, MCT oil, and stevia, if using, in a blender. Blend on high speed for 20 seconds.
2. Divide the tea among four 10-oz or larger glasses, drop 2 ice cubes into each glass.

LOW-CARB COLADA

SERVINGS: 2 | PREP TIME: 5 min. | COOK TIME: none

CARBS: 5.1 g | FAT: 23 g | PROTEIN: 1.5 g | CALORIES: 215

INGREDIENTS

- 1⅓ cups full-fat coconut milk
- 2 oz dark rum (optional)
- 2 Tbsp piña colada–flavored omega oil
- 2 Tbsp MCT oil
- 2 tsp apple cider vinegar
- 4 to 8 drops liquid stevia
- 4 cups ice cubes

DIRECTIONS

1. Blend all ingredients in a blender on high speed until the ice is crushed and the mixture is smooth. You may have to start and stop your blender, pushing the ingredients into the blades.
2. Divide the drink among four 8-ounce glasses and enjoy immediately.

FRESH LEMONADE

SERVINGS: 4 | PREP TIME: 3 min. | COOK TIME: none

CARBS: 2.7 g | FAT: 0.7 g | PROTEIN: 0.7 g | CALORIES: 21

INGREDIENTS

- 4 cups water
- ⅓ cup lemon juice
- ¼ tsp finely ground Himalayan rock salt
- 4 to 6 drops liquid stevia (optional)
- 1 cup ice cubes, for serving
- Fresh mint leaves, for garnish (optional)
- 1 lemon, sliced thin, for serving (optional)

DIRECTIONS

1. Place the water, lemon juice, salt, and stevia (if using) in a liquid-safe container such as a mason jar. Cover and give it a little shake.
2. When ready to drink the lemonade, transfer to a drinking glass and add ice. If desired, top with a couple of mint leaves and serve with lemon slices.

ENERGETIC ICED COFFEE

SERVINGS: 2 | PREP TIME: 5 min. | COOK TIME: none

CARBS: 4.5 g | FAT: 22.3 g | PROTEIN: 5.2 g | CALORIES: 267

INGREDIENTS

- 1¾ cups chilled brewed coffee (regular or decaf)
- 1 Tbsp plus 1 tsp unsweetened smooth almond butter
- Tbsp hulled hemp seeds
- 1 Tbsp MCT oil
- ¼ tsp vanilla extract or powder
- ¼ tsp ground cinnamon
- 2 to 4 drops liquid stevia (optional)
- Pinch of finely ground Himalayan rock salt (optional)
- 4-6 ice cubes

DIRECTIONS

1. Put all the ingredients except the ice in a blender and mix until smooth.
2. Pour into a glass or mason jar, drop in the ice cubes, and enjoy!

SUMMER SMOOTHIE

SERVINGS: 1 | PREP TIME: 5 min. | COOK TIME: 5 min.

CARBS: 7.5 g | FAT: 38.6 g | PROTEIN: 23 g | CALORIES: 449

INGREDIENTS

- ½ cup coconut milk or heavy whipping cream
- ½ cup almond milk
- 1 tablespoon MCT oil
- 1 vanilla bean or 1 tsp unsweetened vanilla extract
- ¼ cup raspberries, blackberries, or strawberries, fresh or frozen
- ¼ cup whey protein
- 3-4 ice cubes

DIRECTIONS

1. Wash the berries. Place everything into a blender and pulse until smooth.

CONCLUSION

Thank you for reading this book and having the patience to try the recipes.

I do hope that you have had as much enjoyment reading and experimenting with the meals as I have had writing the book.

Stay safe and healthy!

RECIPE INDEX

A

Almond Ice Cream 31
Apricot Sherbet...................................47
Avocado Sorbet 39

B

Banana Flavored Ice Cream 16
Blackberry Buttermilk Ice Cream 9
Blackberry Ice Cream........................... 8
Blueberry Ice Cream 10

C

Cherry Flavored Chocolate Ice Cream...26
Chocolate Avocado Ice Cream 24
Chocolate Frosty.................................23
Chunky Nutty Ice Cream 27
Coconut Ice Cream 12
Coconut Milk Fudge Pops 41
Coffee Ice Cream.................................37
Creamier Raspberry Ice Cream............11
Creamy Ice Cream 34
Creamy Lemon Ice Cream 13

E

Egg Free Green Tea Ice Cream 33
Egg Free Vanilla Ice Cream 32
Energetic Iced Coffee..........................52

F

Fresh Lemonade 51
Fruit Sherbet 40

H

Hazelnut Mocha Ice Cream 28

I

Iced Omega Tea 49
Iced Tea 48
Irish Cream Ice Cream.........................35

L

Lime Ice Cream 21
Low-Carb Colada................................50

M

Mint Chocolate Ice Cream...................36

P

Peach Ice Cream................................. 14
Peanut Butter Ice Cream 29
Pecan Ice Cream.................................30
Pumpkin Ice Cream 20

R

Raspberry Ice Cream 15
Raspberry Sherbet..............................44

S

Simple Chocolate Ice Cream 22
Strawberry Cheesecake Ice Cream 18
Strawberry Cheesecake Pops 43
Strawberry Coconut Ice Cream 19
Strawberry Ice Cream......................... 17
Summer Smoothie..............................53

V

Vanilla Bean Semifreddo 45
Vanilla Sherbet....................................46
Vanilla-Almond Ice Pops......................42
Vegan Chocolate Ice Cream 25

Z

Ziplock Bag Ice Cream........................38

CONVERSION TABLES

Dry Weights

oz	Tbsp	C	g	lb
1/2 oz	1 Tbsp	1/16 C	15 g	
1 oz	2 Tbsp	1/8 C	28 g	
2 oz	4 Tbsp	1/4 C	57 g	
3 oz	6 Tbsp	1/3 C	85 g	
4 oz	8 Tbsp	1/2 C	115 g	1/4 lb
8 oz	16 Tbsp	1 C	227 g	1/2 lb
12 oz	24 Tbsp	1 1/2 C	340 g	3/4 lb
16 oz	32 Tbsp	2 C	455 g	1 lb

Liquid Conversions

1 Gallon: 4 quarts, 8 pints, 16 cups, 128 fl oz, 3.8 liters

1 Quart: 2 pints, 4 cups, 32 fl oz, 0.95 liters

1 Pint: 2 cups, 16 fl oz, 480 ml

1 Cup: 16 Tbsp, 8 fl oz, 240 ml

oz	tsp	Tbsp	mL	C	Pt	Qt
1 oz	6 tsp	2 Tbsp	30 ml	1/8 C		
2 oz	12 tsp	4 Tbsp	60 ml	1/4 C		
2 2/3 oz	16 tsp	5 Tbsp	80 ml	1/3 C		
4 oz	24 tsp	8 Tbsp	120 ml	1/2 C		
5 1/3 oz	32 tsp	11 Tbsp	160 ml	2/3 C		
6 oz	36 tsp	12 Tbsp	177 ml	3/4 C		
8 oz	48 tsp	16 Tbsp	237 ml	1 C	1/2 pt	1/4 qt
16 oz	96 tsp	32 Tbsp	480 ml	2 C	1 pt	1/2 qt
32 oz	192 tsp	64 Tbsp	950 ml	4 C	2 pt	1 qt

Fahrenheit to Celcius (F to C)

500 F = 260 C
475 F = 245 C
450 F = 235 C
425 F = 220 C
400 F = 205 C
375 F = 190 C
350 F = 180 C
325 F = 160 C
300 F = 150 C
275 F = 135 C
250 F = 120 C
225 F = 107 C

1 tsp: 5 ml

1 Tbsp: 15 ml

Safe Cooking Meat Temperatures

Minimum temperatures:

USDA Safe at 145 F — Beef Steaks, Briskets, and Roasts; Pork Chops, Roasts, Ribs, Shoulders, and Butts; Lamb Chops, Legs, and Roasts; Fresh Hams, Veal Steaks, Fish, and Shrimp

USDA Safe at 160 F — Ground Meats (except poultry)

USDA Safe at 165 F — Chicken & Turkey, ground or whole